flash fiction

mix-and-match
writing prompts

"This is a very useful manual. With very simple instructions and picking a word from each of the lists, you will build sentences that serve as inspiration for a book, a short story, or even a scene that's calling for some spark. We have lots of fun using it in our weekly writers group. It's a flash of imagination."

— Lourdes Diaz

"*Flash Fiction* is a 'must-have' for writers. Corrine serves the ideas on a silver platter through these inexhaustible lists. I have written dozens of stories due to this gem that sits on my night table. 'Writer's block' no longer has to be part of your vocabulary. You want to write? Here are the prompts, now GO!"

— Pilar Uribe

Version 2
June 2016

ISBN-13: 978-1532937217
ISBN-10: 1532937210

Cover images by Luis Molinero Martínez

instructions

Don't waste time waiting for story ideas to come to you. Flip through this booklet, and you can create characters and plots in seconds.

Simply choose a word or phrase from each section, in order, and then turn those selections into a sentence. It's easy, because the sections are arranged like parts of speech.

Here's a sample prompt to show you how it works.

1.	descriptions (adjectives)	*vengeful*
2.	characters (nouns)	*historian*
3.	actions (verbs)	*steals*
4.	plot twists (objects)	*movie script*
5.	places (more nouns)	*coffee shop*

Add a few articles and prepositions, and you have a premise for a story: *A vengeful historian steals a movie script in a coffee shop.*

Feel free to make changes, substitutions, and additions. You might find a garbage man in the list — but you'll soon discover that your garbage man is actually a garbage woman, or a trash-picking hobo, or an environmentally sensitive vampire who sleeps in a landfill. Let your characters drive the story

You can also play fast and loose with the grammar. You're welcome to turn nouns into verbs, or objects into adjectives. Maybe your character isn't a ghost. Maybe he's just ghostly.

You can change verb conjugations, too. If your hero isn't inflicting wounds, for example, maybe he's the one being wounded.

Make the most of the suggestions in this booklet. Remember that they're starting points, not final destinations. With any luck, they'll take you into a story that practically writes itself.

— Corrine Kenner

contents

1. descriptions

absent-minded
abusive
accident-prone
acerbic
activist
adolescent
adventurous
African
aging
agoraphobic
alcoholic
allergy-prone
amnesiac
ancient
androgynous
angry
annoyed
anorexic
antagonistic
anxiety-ridden
apathetic
apprentice
arrogant
artistic
Asian
aspiring
assistant
athletic
Australian
autistic
award-winning
badass
bald
bankrupt
bashful
battle-weary

bearded
beaten
befuddled
beloved
bewildered
bilingual
birth-marked
bisexual
bleach-blonde
blind
blonde
bored
bored
brain-damaged
Brazilian
Buddhist
budding
bullied
bustling
calculating
camera-shy
Canadian
cannibalistic
carefree
careless
Catholic
caveman
celebrity
chain-smoking
champion
charming
cheerful
childless
childless
Chinese
Christian

chronically late
cigar-chomping
cigarette-
  smoking
civilian
classless
claustrophobic
clubfooted
clueless
clumsy
communist
compulsive
conceited
concerned
condemned
confused
conservative
converted
corpulent
corrupt
crazed
criminal
cruel
crusading
curious
curmudgeonly
deaf
defective
deformed
delinquent
depressed
devilish
diabetic
diligent
disagreeable
diseased

dishonest
disillusioned
distracted
disturbed
divorced
doddering
domineering
door-to-door
drug-addicted
drunk
dwarf
dying
effeminate
elderly
embarrassed
energetic
enthusiastic
envious
evangelical
exotic
extraterrestrial
faithful
fanatical
fascist
fast-talking
fearful
fearless
feeble
foolish
foreign
forgetful
foul-mouthed
fragile
freckled
freelance
free-wheeling

frugal	illegitimate	master	paralyzed
frustrated	illiterate	mean-spirited	paranoid
fumbling	immigrant	menopausal	pathological
fundamentalist	immortal	Mexican	patriotic
gay	impoverished	Middle Eastern	paunchy
gender-fluid	incompetent	military	peace-loving
gentle	incontinent	mindless	penitent
giant	indecisive	miserly	penny-pinching
gluttonous	Indian	money-hungry	perfectionist
gossipy	inept	moody	perfectionistic
government	inexperienced	moralistic	phlegmy
graceful	innocent	morbidly obese	phobic
greedy	insomniac	murderous	photogenic
grouchy	introverted	musclebound	pockmarked
grubby	invisible	muscular	polygamous
grumpy	irritating	musical	pot-bellied
guileless	Islamic	Muslim	pot-smoking
guilt-ridden	Itinerant	mute	pregnant
gum-chewing	Japanese	naïve	prehistoric
handicapped	jealous	narcissistic	prejudiced
hapless	jealous	Native	professorial
hard-driving	Jewish	American	promiscuous
hardened	juvenile	needy	pudgy
hard-hearted	lactose-	newly single	punch drunk
hard-working	intolerant	nostalgic	pushy
harried	lazy	novice	puzzled
hate-filled	lesbian	nymphomaniac	racist
hedonistic	lonely	obnoxious	rageful
helpful	long-winded	obscene	rambunctious
hermit	loud-mouthed	obsequious	rebellious
homeless	loutish	obsessive	reclusive
homesick	lovesick	old-fashioned	recovering
homophobic	love-struck	one-armed	red-faced
hopeless	macho	one-eyed	redheaded
horny	maimed	ordinary	reincarnated
hunchbacked	malicious	orphaned	religious
husky	married	Orthodox	reluctant
hypochondriac	masculine	overweight	renegade
illegal	masked	overworked	reserved

rogue
runaway
rural
Russian
rustic
ruthless
sassy
Scandinavian
scarred
scheming
scientific
scowling
secret
seductive
selective
self-conscious
self-righteous
sentimental
sex-crazed
sexy
shadowy
shaggy
shaky
shallow
shape-shifting
short-tempered
shriveled
shy
sickly

single
six-fingered
skeptical
sleepy
sloppy
smirking
smooth-talking
sneaky
snobby
socialist
sociopath
soft-hearted
soft-hearted
soft-spoken
South
  American
Southern
spicy
spiteful
spoiled
squeamish
standoffish
starving
statuesque
steampunk
stubborn
stuttering
substitute
successful

suicidal
sulky
sunburned
surly
sweaty
sycophantic
tall
tattooed
teenage
tense
thoughtful
thoughtless
time-traveling
toothless
tortured
touring
transgendered
transsexual
transvestite
trashy
travelling
treacherous
tricky
two-timing
unassuming
undead
undercover
underpaid
underwater

underweight
unemployed
unlicensed
unmarried
unshaven
urban
vacuous
vain
vegan
vegetarian
vengeful
Victorian
vindictive
violent
vivacious
voiceless
wandering
weak-willed
wealthy
widowed
wiry
witty
wizened
world-famous
worldly
wounded
wrathful
wrinkled
youthful

2. characters

accountant
acrobat
activist
actor
adulterer
air traffic controller
alchemist
alien
ambulance driver
amputee
android
angel
anthropologist
appliance repairer
archeologist
architect
armchair tourist
artist
assassin
astrologer
astronaut
astronomer
athlete
attorney
audiologist
author
babysitter
bachelor
bag boy
bank teller
barber
bartender
beach bum
beautician
beauty queen
bee keeper

bellman
belly dancer
benefactor
bibliophile
billionaire
biologist
birdwatcher
bishop
black widow
blacksmith
body double
bodyguard
bookkeeper
border guard
boxer
boy band
boy genius
brain surgeon
bricklayer
bride
builder
building inspector
bully
bureaucrat
burglar
burn victim
bus driver
butcher
butler
cab driver
cabana boy
cable guy
call girl
car mechanic
carnival barker
carpenter

carpet layer
cartoonist
cashier
casket maker
cat burglar
cat lady
chauffeur
cheerleader
chef
chemist
chess player
child star
chimney sweep
chiropractor
choreographer
circus freak
circus performer
civil servant
clone
clown
coach
coin collector
comedian
communist
composer
compulsive hoarder
con man
concierge
conductor
congressman
conservationist
construction worker
consultant
contractor
convict
cook

coroner	escaped felon	grandmother
cosmetologist	evangelist	Greek god
cosmonaut	executioner	grocer
cowboy	exhibitionist	groom
crack addict	exterminator	groupie
crackhead	farmer	guitarist
crone	farmer's daughter	gym teacher
dancer	fashion designer	gymnast
debutante	fashionista	gypsy
demon	father	hair stylist
dentist	feminist	hangman
designer	femme fatale	health inspector
desk clerk	financial planner	hermit
detective	firefighter	high-school
devil	fisherman	sweethearts
dictator	fishmonger	hired man
dietician	fitness trainer	historian
dinner guest	flight attendant	hit man
disc jockey	forklift operator	hitchhiker
dishwasher	fortuneteller	hobo
dispatcher	fugitive	homeless person
dockworker	funeral director	hostage negotiator
doctor	furniture upholsterer	hula dancer
dog catcher	gambler	human cannonball
dog walker	gang member	hunter
doorman	gangster	hypnotist
double agent	garbage man	hypochondriac
dressmaker	gardener	identity thief
drug addict	geneticist	informant
drug dealer	genie	insurance agent
drummer	geologist	interpreter
economist	germophobe	inventor
editor	ghost	investor
efficiency expert	godfather	ironworker
electrician	godmother	jailor
elevator operator	golf pro	janitor
embezzler	good Samaritan	jeweler
engineer	governor	journalist
environmentalist	grandfather	judge

juggler
junkie
knight
lab technician
landscaper
lawyer
leprechaun
librarian
life coach
lifeguard
limo driver
loan officer
loan shark
longshoreman
lothario
love child
lumberjack
lunch lady
machinist
madman
magician
maid
mailman
male model
manicurist
masseuse
mathematician
mayor
mechanic
mermaid
messenger
meteorologist
meter reader
milkman
millionaire
mind reader
mobster
model
monk

mortician
mother
mother-in-law
motorcycle cop
mountain climber
movie star
mummy
museum curator
musician
mutant
negotiator
newlyweds
news junkie
novelist
nuclear scientist
nun
nurse
Olympian
one-hit wonder
optometrist
orphan
orthodontist
painter
pall bearer
parachutist
paralegal
paramedic
parole officer
parolee
party planner
peeping tom
performer
pharmacist
philanderer
philosopher
photographer
physical therapist
physicist
physiologist

pianist
pickpocket
pilot
pimp
pioneer
pirate
plastic surgeon
plumber
podiatrist
poet
police officer
politician
pool boy
pop star
pope
pornographer
preacher
priest
prince
princess
principal
prison guard
private eye
professional
  organizer
professor
programmer
proofreader
prostitute
psychiatrist
psychic
psychopath
public relations pro
publisher
rabbi
rancher
rapper
real estate agent
receptionist

recruiter	software engineer	tour guide
repairman	soldier	tourist
reporter	soldier of fortune	traitor
robot	sommelier	trapeze artist
rock star	songwriter	treasure hunter
rocket scientist	speech pathologist	tree surgeon
romance writer	spinster	tree trimmer
roofer	spirit guide	truck driver
royalty	spy	typesetter
sailor	stage mother	undercover cop
salesperson	stalker	undertaker
scientist	stamp collector	used car salesman
scuba diver	starlet	usher
sculptor	statistician	vampire
seamstress	stenographer	vaudevillian
secret agent	stepmother	veterinarian
secretary	stock clerk	video editor
security guard	stockbroker	Viking
senator	stormtrooper	virgin
servant	street preacher	voyeur
settler	stripper	waiter
sharpshooter	surfer	waitress
ship's captain	surgeon	warlock
shipping clerk	surveyor	weather chaser
shock jock	swimsuit model	web developer
shoe salesman	synchronized	wedding planner
shopkeeper	swimmer	welder
sideshow barker	tailor	werewolf
singer	tarot reader	wet nurse
single mother	tax collector	widow
slave	taxi driver	window washer
slumlord	teacher	witch
smuggler	technical writer	witch hunter
sniper	technophobe	wood nymph
social worker	teenager	world's tallest man
socialist	television host	wrestler
socialite	tennis coach	writer
sociologist	tennis pro	yoga instructor
sociopath	terrorist	zookeeper

3. actions

abandons
abducts
accuses
admires
adopts
advises
agrees
alleges
analyzes
announces
annoys
apologizes
applauds
argues
arrests
assassinates
attacks
attends
auditions
avenges
backs into
bans
begs
betrays
blackmails
blinds
bombs
brainwashes
breaks
bribes
bruises
bumps
burns
buys
calculates
calls

campaigns
cancels
captures
challenges
chokes
chooses
claims
clashes
coaches
collects
collides
compliments
confesses
confuses
connects
copies
corrects
cracks
craves
crawls
crushes
debates
deceives
deciphers
delivers
destroys
diagnoses
disables
disappears
disapproves
discovers
disguises
disrupts
donates
doubts
drops

earns
emails
embarrasses
embezzles
employs
enchants
encounters
enters
entraps
erases
evades
examines
explores
fears
fights
films
finds
flattens
flees
flirts
floats
foils
folds
forgets
frames
frightens
gambles
gets caught
gets lost
gossips
guards
heals
helps
hijacks
hitchhikes
hooks

hopes
identifies
ignores
imagines
impersonates
impresses
imprisons
infects
informs
inherits
injures
instructs
insults
intercepts
interferes
interrupts
introduces
invades
invents
investigates
invites
joins
juggles
kicks
kidnaps
kidnaps
kills
kisses
lands
laughs
launches
learns
leaves
libels
listens
longs for

loses	pulls	serves	tames
loves	punches	settles	terrifies
lusts after	punishes	shares	testifies
mails	pursues	shelters	tests
marries	pushes	shocks	threatens
measures	questions	shoots	touches
meets	races	shops	tours
misleads	realizes	signals	trades
misses	receives	sins	trains
moves	recognizes	slanders	transports
murders	records	sleeps with	traps
nails	reflects	smashes	travels
notices	refuses	smiles	tricks
observes	rejects	smuggles	tries
obsesses	relaxes	sparks	troubles
obtains	remembers	spoils	trusts
offends	removes	squashes	tugs
opens	repairs	squeals	twists
orders	replies	squeezes	undermines
ostracizes	requests	stabs	undresses
overdoses	rescues	stains	unfastens
overhears	revives	stalks	visits
overpowers	risks	starts	waits
picks	robs	steals	wants
plans	robs	steers	warns
plays	ruins	stops	washes
plots	rules	strengthens	watches
poisons	scatters	stretches	weakens
postpones	scratches	strips	welcomes
preaches	seals	suffers	wishes
preserves	searches	surprises	wrestles
pretends	seduces	suspects	writes
propositions	seeks	suspends	

4. plot twists

abduction
accusation
adoption
alarm bells
alien invasion
allegation
alternate timeline
amnesia
animal attack
animal bite
arch rival
arrest
arrest warrant
artifact
assassination attempt
attack
audition
avalanche
baby in a basket
backstage pass
ball game
barroom brawl
biker gang
birth
blackout
blind date
blizzard
body double
bomb threat
bombing
book burning
brainwashing
bridge collapse
broadcast
buried treasure
bush crash

calendar
car wreck
cave-in
celebrity
cell phone
championship
chemical weapons
civil war
collapse
coma
conspiracy
contest
corpse
court hearing
court summons
credit card
crime family
crime scene
criminal charge
crown jewels
dead body
dead president
death match
death sentence
death threat
death wish
debate
dementia
diamond ring
disguise
drive-by shooting
drought
drug deal
drug overdose
drug stash
duel

dying wish
earthquake
election
elixir of life
email
epidemic
evacuation
excavation
explosion
exposé
fire alarm
fire drill
flash mob
flood
fountain of youth
future self
ghost
golden ticket
gossip
government plot
government secret
gunshot
hallucination
haunting
heart attack
hidden doorway
hidden world
historical figure
hostage
hurricane
identical twin
imposter
infestation
injection
insect bite
insurance claim

invasion	older self	secret room
investigation	one-night stand	secret society
invisible ink	overdose	seduction
invitation	pandemic	seizure
keyring	panic	sex scandal
kidnapping	parallel universe	shooting
landslide	paranoia	sinkhole
last will and	photo album	sirens
testament	plague	spell book
last-minute warning	plane crash	spirit
lawsuit	plane ticket	spy ring
lie	plastic surgery	stabbing
lightning strike	plea for help	stalker
long-lost relative	poison	stampede
lost child	political campaign	stolen car
lottery ticket	power outage	stolen passport
love at first sight	press conference	storm
lucky charm	presumed dead	suicide pact
magic glasses	promotion	superpower
magic lamp	proposition	surgery
magic pen	protest	talking cat
manila envelope	radioactive spill	telegram
manuscript	ransom note	temptation
map	rebellion	terrorist attack
marriage proposal	reunion	text message
medical mystery	revelation	three wishes
message in a bottle	riot	thunderstorm
million dollars	robbery	ticking time bomb
miracle cure	robot	time travel
misdelivered mail	roll of film	tombstone
mistaken identity	runestone	tornado
monster	scandal	tour
movie script	secret admirer	train wreck
murder weapon	secret code	trap
musical instrument	secret diary	treasure chest
mysterious package	secret enemy	treasure map
mythic creature	secret formula	trial
news story	secret garden	tsunami
obituary	secret passage	unmailed letter

uprising
urgent letter
video
virus
wakes from a coma

war plans
warning lights
weapons stockpile
wild animal
wildfire

wrong number
x-ray glasses
younger self
zombie invasion

5. settings

Africa
aircraft carrier
airplane
airport
antique shop
apartment
aquarium
archeological dig
art gallery
art studio
Asia
attic
auction
auditorium
Australia
award ceremony
baby shower
back room
bakery
balcony
ballroom
bank
baptism
bar
bar/bat mitzvah
barge
barn
barracks
baseball field
basement
basketball court
bathhouse
bathroom
bathtub
battle
battlefield

beach
beauty parlor
bedroom
bingo parlor
birthday party
blacksmith shop
blimp
blizzard
blood drive
boardwalk
boat
bomb shelter
bonfire
bookstore
border
bridal shower
bridge
bris
buffet
bull run
bungalow
burning building
butcher shop
butterfly garden
cabin
cafeteria
cage
campground
Canada
candle shop
canoe
canyon
car crash
carnival
carpentry shop
casino

castle
cathedral
cave
cellar
chalet
chapel
charity ball
chateau
chess match
Chicago
chicken coop
China
church
circus
city hall
class reunion
classroom
cliff
clinic
clubhouse
coal mine
cocktail party
coffee shop
competition
computer store
concert
condominium
conference
confessional
convention
cottage
courthouse
courtroom
crack house
craft store
crematorium

cruise ship
crypt
customs office
Dallas
dance
dentist chair
Denver
department store
desert
Detroit
dialysis center
diner
dining room
disco
double-decker bus
doughnut shop
dressing room
drive-through
drugstore
dump
dungeon
earthquake
Egypt
Eiffel Tower
engagement party
escalator
estate
Europe
factory
fallout shelter
family reunion
Fargo
farm
farmers market
farmhouse
fashion show
Ferris wheel
festival
film festival

finish line
firehouse
fitness center
flower shop
food truck
football field
forest
fortress
freeway
fruit stand
fun house
fundraiser
funeral
furniture store
game show
garage
garage sale
garden
gas station
ghetto
glacier
golf course
graduation
graveyard
Greece
greenhouse
grocery store
guitar shop
gym
hacienda
hair salon
happy hour
harvest festival
hat shop
heaven
hell
high-rise
highway
hippodrome

history center
holiday party
home office
honeymoon
hospital
hostel
hot-air balloon
hotel
hovel
hunting lodge
hurricane
hut
ice arena
ice floe
ice-cream parlor
igloo
Indian reservation
inn
international date line
island
jail
jungle
junkyard
kiosk
kissing booth
kitchen
labyrinth
Las Vegas
library
light house
lion's den
liquor store
living room
locker room
log cabin
London
Los Angeles
lunchroom
mailroom

mall
manor
mansion
marathon
Mars colony
massage parlor
meadow
Mexico
Miami
midnight mass
mint
monastery
monsoon
morgue
Moscow
mosque
motel
mountain
movie theater
museum
Nashville
nature preserve
New Orleans
New York
newsroom
nightclub
north pole
nudist colony
nursery
observatory
ocean
Octoberfest
office
oil rig
Old West
opium den
orange grove
orchestra hall
orchestra pit

orphanage
outer space
outhouse
pageant
pagoda
palace
pancake house
parade
Paris
parking lot
party
pawn shop
peep show
penthouse
pep rally
Phoenix
picnic
pier
pirate ship
pizza shop
plane crash
planetarium
plantation
playground
poker game
polling place
pool
post office
prom
protest march
pub
pyramid
quicksand
racetrack
radio station
railroad
rainstorm
ranch
reception

record store
red carpet
renaissance fair
resort
rest stop
restaurant
restroom
Rio de Janeiro
riverboat
rock concert
roller coaster
rooftop garden
rose garden
Russia
sailboat
saloon
sandwich shop
school
school bus
science museum
sculpture garden
seashore
Seattle
shack
shanty
shed
shoe store
sideshow
sidewalk
silo
skyscraper
slum
snow storm
sod hut
South America
South Pole
space station
spaceship
speakeasy

stadium
stairwell
state park
steakhouse
stockyard
storage unit
storeroom
street car
street fair
strip club
sub shop
submarine
subway
suite
summer camp
surprise party
swamp
swimming pool
tabernacle
taco truck
tanning bed

tattoo parlor
tavern
taxi
tea parlor
teepee
television studio
temple
tenement
theater
thrift shop
tour bus
townhouse
toxic waste dump
toy shop
train
train station
tree farm
treehouse
tunnel
tunnel of love
university

van
vending machine
vet's office
villa
village square
vineyard
volcano
voting booth
wake
walk-in freezer
warehouse
warplane
warship
water cooler
wedding
whorehouse
yacht
yurt
zephyr
zoo

character names

Sometimes the trickiest part of writing flash fiction is coming up with character names. Here's a list, so you can grab and go. Feel free to shorten or combine the names, change spellings, use nicknames, or add male, female, and foreign variations.

Aaron	Bart	Cecelia	Dewey
Abraham	Beatrice	Cecil	Diana
Ace	Benjamin	Celeste	Dick
Ada	Bernard	Charity	Doc
Adam	Bernice	Charles	Dog
Addie	Bert	Cherry	Donald
Adeline	Bertha	Chester	Dora
Adolph	Bessie	Clara	Doris
Agnes	Betty	Clarence	Dorothy
Alan	Beulah	Claudine	Dot
Albert	Bill	Clayton	Douglas
Alberta	Bird	Cleo	Earl
Alex	Blanche	Cliff	Earnest
Alfred	Blondie	Clyde	Ed
Alice	Blossom	Constance	Edgar
Alvin	Bluebell	Consuela	Edith
Alyssa	Bo	Cora	Edmund
Amanda	Bob	Cornelius	Edna
Amelia	Bonnie	Corrine	Edward
Amos	Boots	Coyla	Edwin
Amy	Boss	Craig	Effie
Andrew	Buddy	Curtis	Elbert
Anne	Bugsy	Dahlia	Eleanor
Anthony	Butch	Daisy	Elizabeth
Archie	Calla	Daisy	Ella
Arnold	Calvin	Daniel	Ellen
Art	Camellia	Darren	Elmer
Audrey	Cari	David	Elsie
August	Carmine	Della	Elvira
Babe	Carolyn	Dennis	Emil

Emily	Gordon	Jacob	Leroy
Emmett	Grace	Jake	Leslie
Eric	Gus	James	Lester
Erma	Guy	Jan	Lewis
Essie	Hank	Janice	Lilac
Estelle	Hannah	Jasmine	Lillian
Esther	Hans	Jason	Lily
Ethel	Harold	Jayne	Lizzie
Etta	Harry	Jean	Lloyd
Eugene	Harvey	Jeff	Lois
Eula	Hattie	Jenny	Lola
Eunice	Hazel	Jerome	Lon
Eva	Helen	Jerry	Lottie
Evelyn	Helge	Jesse	Louis
Everett	Henry	Jesus	Louise
Faith	Herbert	Jim	Lourdes
Fannie	Herman	Joe	Lucille
Felix	Hilda	Joelene	Lula
Fern	Hillary	John	Luther
Fernando	Homer	Juan	Lydia
Flora	Hope	Juanita	Lynn
Florence	Horace	Judas	Mack
Flossie	Howard	Julia	Madeline
Floyd	Hubert	Julio	Mae
Francis	Hugh	Juniper	Magda
Frank	Hyacinth	Katherine	Maggie
Freckles	Ida	Keanu	Magnolia
Fred	Ina	Kenneth	Malcolm
Frederick	Inez	Knut	Margie
Frieda	Ira	Larry	Maria
Geneva	Irene	Laura	Marigold
Genevieve	Iris	Laurel	Marilyn
George	Irma	Lavender	Mark
Gerald	Irvin	Lawrence	Marlys
Gertrude	Irving	Lee	Marshall
Gilbert	Isaac	Lela	Martha
Gladys	Isabelle	Lena	Marvin
Gloria	Ivy	Leo	Mary
Goldie	Jack	Leonard	Matthew

Maurice	Oscar	Royal	Tempest
Max	Otis	Ruby	Thelma
Melvin	Otto	Rudy	Theodore
Mike	Pansy	Rufus	Theresa
Mildred	Patricia	Ruth	Thor
Milton	Patrick	Sadie	Tiny
Minnie	Paul	Sage	Tom
Miriam	Pauline	Sally	Tony
Molly	Pearl	Salvador	Tulip
Moose	Peggy	Sam	Velma
Morris	Penelope	Samantha	Vera
Myrtle	Peony	Sarah	Vernon
Naomi	Percy	Sasha	Veronica
Nathan	Peter	Scott	Victor
Nathaniel	Petunia	Sidney	Viola
Nell	Philip	Simon	Violet
Nelson	Phyllis	Sis	Virgil
Nettie	Pilar	Slim	Virginia
Nicholas	Poppy	Sophia	Vivian
Nina	Pops	Spud	Wallace
Nora	Prudence	Stan	Walter
Norma	Rachel	Stella	Wayne
Norman	Ralph	Stephen	Wesley
Olga	Raven	Steve	Wilbur
Olive	Red	Studs	William
Oliver	Richard	Sully	Wilma
Ollie	Robert	Susan	Winifred
Opal	Roger	Sylvester	Zaria
Ora	Roosevelt	Sylvia	Zinnia
Orchid	Rosie	Ted	Zippy
Orville	Roy	Temperance	Zed

additional tips and hints

- Look for story ideas and combinations that amuse and intrigue you — even if they seem far-fetched.
- Set a timer, and push yourself to write scenes or stories in 10- or 15-minute bursts.
- Create more complex stories by choosing additional plot elements. You can double up on descriptions, too.
- Compile an entire cast of characters, each with their own quirks and foibles.
- Write like you talk, and pretend that you're talking to a friend.
- Don't reach for words or phrases that you wouldn't use in ordinary conversation.
- If you can't think of the word you want to use, substitute a placeholder or leave a blank space, and keep writing.
- Let your imagination run wild. Don't edit yourself while you're writing.
- Don't censor yourself, either. You're writing fiction — so feel free to lie, exaggerate, twist the truth, and unleash your demons.
- Share this booklet with your writers group. Develop a prompt together, and then compare the stories you write.
- Take this booklet on the road, and use it in combination with other sources of inspiration — like paintings and photographs in a museum, or overheard conversations in a coffee shop.
- If you're in a busy area, and you're distracted by sights and sounds you can't ignore, write them into the story.
- Write in this booklet. Start by adding your own character names. List the names of everyone in your family, including their middle names and nicknames — and for variety, go back several generations. You can also list the names of your friends, neighbors, coworkers, pets, old roommates, former lovers, and sworn and secret enemies.
- Post your stories on your website, blog, or social media page, and send me a link! My email address is *corrine@corrinekenner.com*.

about the author

Corrine Kenner has written more than 20 books, which have been translated into 12 languages. She's also a former newspaper reporter and magazine editor. You can find her work on Amazon, in Barnes & Noble bookstores, and in shops around the world.

Corrine was raised on a farm in North Dakota. As a student, she lived in Brazil, where she learned Portuguese, and Los Angeles, where she earned a degree in philosophy from California State University.

She now lives in Florida with her husband Dan. Together, they have four daughters, three cats, and a dog who can sing.

For classes and coaching with Corrine, call 800.737.7864 or visit corrinekenner.com.

also by corrine kenner

Astrology for Writers
Tarot for Writers
Tarot Journaling
Tarot and Astrology
Simple Fortunetelling with Tarot Cards
Tall Dark Stranger: Tarot for Romance
Crystals for Beginners
Strange But True
The Ghosts of Devils Lake
The Colors of Light: A Guide to the Impressionist Tarot
The Epicurean Tarot
The Tarot of Physics
The Wizards Tarot

CPSIA information can be obtained
at www.ICGtesting.com
Printed in the USA
LVOW13s1623110417
530424LV00026B/332/P